Unsaid Thoughts

Deepika Yadav

BookLeaf Publishing

India | USA | UK

Presentation by *BookLeaf Publishing*

Web: www.bookleafpub.com

E-mail: info@bookleafpub.com

ISBN: 9789363319189

First edition 2024

This book is dedicated to those who dare to dream, to those who find solace in words, and to those who believe in the power of storytelling.

Our wavering hearts that fail to let out the words at the right moment or regret having shared some heartbreaking moments.

Welcome to my world of giving ourselves a chance to resonate with our lost selves and to heal on this journey of shades of love, forgiveness, self-finding and healing journey.

This book is for all of you.

Warm regards,

Deepika Yadav

ACKNOWLEDGEMENT

Writing a book is never a solitary endeavor; it is the culmination of support, encouragement, and collaboration from countless individuals. I am deeply grateful to all those who have contributed to the creation of this work.

First and foremost, I extend my heartfelt appreciation to my family for their unwavering love, understanding, and patience throughout this journey. Their support has been my rock, grounding me in times of uncertainty and celebrating with me in moments of triumph.

I extend my gratitude to the publishing team, who have worked tirelessly to bring this book to life. Your dedication and professionalism have transformed my words into a tangible reality.

To the readers, thank you for embarking on this journey with me. Your curiosity, open-mindedness, and willingness to explore new ideas are the driving force behind my writing.

My warmest regards,
Deepika Yadav

PREFACE

Welcome to "Unsaid Thoughts." In these pages, you will embark on a journey through the unspoken corners of the human experience.

Thoughts left unexpressed can weigh heavily on the soul, lingering in the shadows of our consciousness. Yet, within these unsaid thoughts lie profound truths, raw emotions, and untold stories waiting to be unveiled.

As the author of this book, I have endeavored to capture the essence of these unspoken whispers – the words left unsaid, the feelings left unshared, and the stories left untold.

As you turn the pages of this book, may you find solace in the shared experiences of others, comfort in the beauty of vulnerability, and courage to embrace your own unsaid thoughts.

Thank you for joining me on this exploration of the human heart and mind. May our journey together bring light to the shadows and voice to the unsaid.

Warm regards,
Deepika Yadav

TABLE OF CONTENTS

Whispers of the Wood

Clouds are calm as white,
But when in anger, turns grey,
While Nature keeps blooming, what a sight!

When things are not right,
But wish to overcome all fears,
Then to set your heart ablaze is right!

Live in the moment is what they say,
But living in those memories is what I like,
Don't want my feelings to change in a day!

Lotus, the sacred one rising from the mud,
Pristine is the aura of your beauty,
So pure to bring the riches to the ground!

Daffodils are my language of love,
Standing there, holding them in your hands,
Give them to me, I may make a wish for us!

Your Existence!

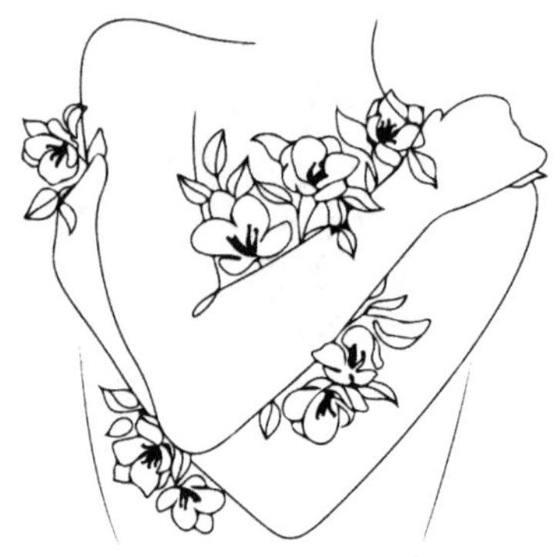

You are undiscovered
Cooed up in solace,

Your beauty, unaware
Soul's wavering to quest,

Your presence, unapproachable
Your unfurled, pristine existence,

So far you are
Say how shall I edge closer,

Your existence to me
Is where my realm of thoughts ends!

Eternal Youth

I'll see you again,
I told myself
When I've learnt to let go of this weight,
And let myself fly.

The eternal youth I seek,
To be freed from this cocoon
To the oceans I've dreamt to discover,
And mountains to explore.

Crossing paths, exchanging lores,
Resting under the trees
Breathing the fresh air that's lost,
Seeking the bliss,
Letting go of my ignorance,
Finding solace in truth.

Pondering as to how nature endures the pain,
I shall Transcend
This physical me that remains elusive,
My Eternal youth may gleam radiantly.

Life is Kinetic

We grow in parts
Our souls have dimensions to enhance,
Our hearts take us back
Where the mind pulls us back to reality,

We all are just different people
Striving to find ourselves,
See within yourself to know your true worth
As seeking is the path to enlightenment,

Endeavor on your journey
Heal yourself and others in the way,
Life is kinetic
Waiting for you to be the change.

The rising sun would wake me up
To the demanding day, that'll be my life!
Will it be cushy to stay?
Or where time is running like crazy…

Wandering to find myself

The soothing breezes that tactual my skin
To the brightened-up sky that soothes my eyes,
The shady trees whispering through leaves
A beautiful way to make wind be heard by us,

Oh! My beautiful bird of paradise and orchids
How much to wander on these island hills,
In search of ecstasy for my soul
Will I be able to find my true self!

What If?

What if our eyes didn't meet that day,
The urge to glance once in some way
Your smile so bright,
It melted me at sight

My troubles washed away
As the sea waves make the sand sway,
Where are hearts flushed with silence,
So as to lighten our gazes so intense

What if we shared our words,
Sweet as some melodies unheard
How much I wished to share stories with you,
Yearning for a bond we could grow

Lest our eyes conveyed enough,
In that silent ballet of ours
With a smile do we depart,
Thinking when would we be brave enough
To let our hearts out.

When He has his Eyes on You

It feels so sweet when he has his eyes on you,
while you are looking away
Just like when we aren't beholding the moon,
It's still staring at us all the time.

Now each breath is sweeter,
Knowing how he feels
Love someone who can adore your flaws,
Yet can clear up the Chaos in your heart ❤

Fear of losing you

Every answer to love's mystery
finds its way to those memories,
At the very moment
when I gather your laughter,
Into every inch of my heart.

You never stop illuminating my world
Without you, my heart sets itself on fire,
Until your touch, would water me enough
When you are not beside me,
Fear of losing you devours my being

Fear plays its game of preying on my heart,
Unless I let my vulnerability win
Nothing can make us apart.
To let your ego and fear leave is better
Than letting the one you love to go.

Illusionary mind

The moments I spent with you,
Take me back in time

The dreams I have of you,
Pull me back in there

Your illusion surrounds my mind,
That revolves and binds my soul

Love is what will hold me when I'm lost,
To stand next to me when I need it most.

You Feel Heavenly

Your lips, my lips
Feels Heavenly
Your eyes saw mine,

A cosmic Celestial
Our hands brushed and intertwined
Such intimacy!

Like the two burning sticks dancing,
Ready to immerse ourselves in the flames of
love
I may fret not, but let my fire go astray!

You and me, two people in love,
In solitude, not pretending to be in love
How beautiful is it, isn't it!

Whispers of Night

My love for you is like fire,
That dares to touch the frozen heart of yours
The fire consumes my pain,
A force that consumes our passion,
making our hearts warmer

Gives way to my desires
Melt those mysteries that surround you
To make us feel suffice
To devour our souls, urging us to be touched
Leaving no corner untouched,

You are strong as ice for me
But watching you stand in solitude
My eyes thirstily await for you to see me
That Craves to burn us with the desire for love
In the Whispers of Night, a beauty untold

This desire for love may never perish,
This passion for tasting love shall never die
That one look, and I can't catch my breath
A wild, untamed fire of tempts and teases,
And I can't help but keep falling for you!

Ruins

Why love is so complicated?
Why am I in ruins?
I want to run away from you,
But you always catch me before I leave
Why am I so attached to your lies,
That even if you lie to my face...

Why does my conscience deny me knowing
your true face?
You don't know; I'm breaking everyday
With your facade of emotions, you show me
I'm ruined and tired of your games
Fed up with weakness called compassion…

If you can't give me a reason to stay,
At least let me go
I've come so far in my dreams with you,

That you, breaking my heart now…
Will definitely break me
Take my innocence away
Feed my soul with scars…

Because loving him was never easy,
Neither it was painless
Why hurt someone you only intend to love,
Should've stayed strangers
It drained me, left hope in me, ruined me,
For love, though fragile, now I'll find my way…

Tears

To not invite them,
Still they roll down my eyes
How much can they bear,
When my heart can't control.

How shall they not fall,
Only to make me realize, there is pain
The warmth they give to my face,
Not your words can feel the same.

They've been there in my sorrow,
Just to see how much darkness can i carry
The more they fall,
The more my fingers slide them away!

So, they may not be seen, not be felt
Whom shall I tell!

That my tears have seen it all…
In devotion, in sadness, in happiness
I'm glad, they've been there.

You broke me Unknowingly

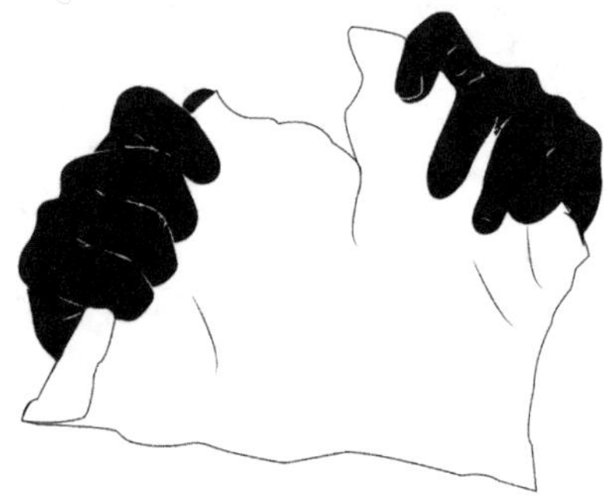

All I only hope for is
That every ounce I drained on you,
Your absence may never break me
No matter how heavy my chest may feel…

I wish not to wither away
When silence roars,
Bringing back the moments of betrayal
Deceived me of myself
Losing to your skin!

I remember, my heart stopped thumping
My world froze just to watch you closely
And in that pause, I saw a gentle you,
Unknowingly fallen for you

With time, when our love confessed
And inch by inch, you lost your interest,
Every day felt like my heart cracked a bit,
You breaking me unknowingly

And now, whatever I have left of me,
I will not let my heart burn to ashes,
I'll water it till it runs with courage again
Cleansing my poisoned soul!

Was it even Worth it?

Is it too hard to explain
That it becomes elusive for your soul
To realize what you lost
When you get it, it's not what it is

You were healing while our hearts walked
And how I felt, oneiric after we talked
Memorising each other's lines
Making us habitual to our signs

Things you said became poetry
Your absence etched in memories
For me, it was difficult to face the reality
Facing reality proved a daunting task for me,

Days went by, taking away years slowly
Being wayward with my choices
Keeping my mind behind my heart
Was it even worth it, I ask...

A Past Relived

A painful past relived,
Surrounds you with innumerable thorns
A beautiful tomorrow you wish to wield,
Commands you to forget what haunts!

My heart's throbbing with desire,
As your fingers grazed my skin
I found you amidst the chaos,
I espied you through a sea of faces…

After all this time, I shall say to you
Symphony of my emotions for you,
Will remain for you, always
But I shall not spoil what I have,
To relive the past.

Wavering Thoughts

The ups and downs,
like waves in the sea
How & what shall I say?
So my words stay hidden inside a shell,
Waiting to burst out…

Should I hear what they say?
I have deep wounds!
I can't speak out? At my own pace, I shall…
Not saying much,
Doesn't mean I have nothing to say

Unaware of my wants,
Just my burdened heart speaks
My thoughts are unspoken.
Don't you think, not all is to be shared with all…
A vessel, holding grief and love

You ask, why so introverted?
This life with limited time seems to not
be able to handle me & my thoughts…
When my heart shakes to the core?
My heart, shaken, broken, used and left,
is there more?

To value the wisdom sorrow brings,
In the depths of despair's darkest hour,
I discover the strength to mend my broken heart.
The lessons, beauty and pain behind it,
The darkness from which I shall rise!

I say, Flaws make me halt?
Losing the time,
due to my created distractions for myself
Much in my soul is left unexplored!
How shall I rise from my troubles, my
unresolved problems!

Shall I rise from them,
Or I bear them or shall I awaken myself?
I think about a lot of things
What if?
Things I wouldn't have done
The things I should've done.

Let the scars heal

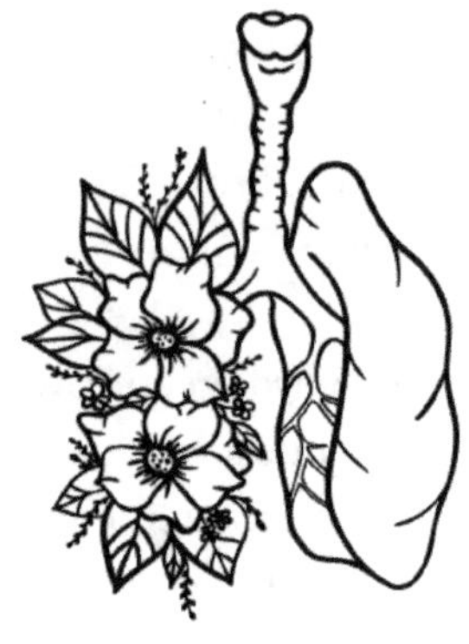

All they see is how calm one is
How have they made it to come so far,
How happy we stay all the time
But what they can't see is my tears that I hide...

The tears and loneliness that surround me
Heaviness of thoughts,
Failing to even decide the easiest stuff…
How have I not been able to grow as a person!

My trust and faith in my God were shaken
It shook so hard, I desperately called for him,
My Krishna came to my rescue, I have him
now…
But the low self-esteem doesn't leave me.

Time ticking by, life running fast,
But here I am, in that closed pot…
Unable to breathe, learning how to survive,
Things I wish to forget…

The pain which I intend to tend,
The story of scars, one day I shall tell
Sins I wish to forgive myself for,
One day, I believe I shall…

Mirror – Your Reflection

From the shy you,
To the bold you

From the unscathed you
To the scarred you

Reflect on what you were
Through the mist and blur

Songs you will write
With the Whispers of your shadow

The Mirror that once gazed at you
Let yourself embrace the true you.

Secrets so deep, untapped
Let the portrait of your soul unwind

From the enchained, fettered and fearful you
Unchain, unshackle and let go

From the staging silence of your eyes
Look at the Mirror with new eyes!

My Lost Confidence

As I walk through the path of wisdom,
Where things seem clear now
I see a light of hope.

It's time I listen to my inner self
Live with grace and some mischief
Assaying what I deserve

When I loved you
I loved you to my fullest,
Like a gentle breeze, I cared
Like a melody of songs I loved…

Walking towards me with steps of compassion
A secret I lost, I shall not disclose
A sigh of relief!

You have now given me what I was looking for
As they say, 'Buds don't bloom before time'
'My confidence', it's you, I was searching for.

And I will be fearless
When I'll let My Confidence own the 'New Me',
And find my own sky to fly in
Leaving in its wake a soul that healed…

The Long Song – Believe and Heal

In this world, I want to be many things,
People tell me I can't be everything
But I shall not listen to what they say,
I'll keep patience, perseverance and dedication
Their envy can't control what I wish to do

Where the river meets the forest,
Let our union be of such beauty
Where the rivers leave the mountains,
Set our hearts free while souls remain intact
Souls know when they connect for the first time
immediately!

With Krishna on my side
I know I can be anything,
I Pray, I Heal a little and then I Grow
And it is my faith that strengthens me.
You are the energy that heals me

Haters can tell me I can't,
Discouragers tell me that I shouldn't
No matter what anyone says,
I believe in myself
As you survived the days you couldn't have
thought of!

Anything I put my mind to,
I know that's what I can do.
No matter what anyone says,
Realising, everybody liked, cared for you,
Until you let everything slide!

No one knows what life has hidden for us,
So keep faith.
Grip up your strengths,
And face your limits.
As pain has already healed you in many ways!

For those who lose faith,
Lose their paths.
It's not always as to follow what the elderly say,
But to make your steps count, do what is right

Stop hurting yourself for those who don't care!

Thee (the almighty) never envies you,
He'll encourage you.
To be what you call out for,
Become what others stop you from being.
As you can start again, over and over…

I shall sing a song for myself
Where pain taught it's value for emotions,
The divine intervention of healing
To calm our souls, we pick up our pens,
To let yourself know, You need you!

Seven minutes

You came into my life like a fairytale
And here, I wish you to be my seven minutes

Innumerable moments to reminisce about
Wrapped up in your arms, collecting memories

Our first kiss, first date, first long ride
To the day, you calling me yours

The breaths we shared in a lovely home
The invisible red thread that ties us

In those last seven minutes
You'll be there in my most searched memoirs

July

As July comes to an end
Let's hope for the other half
has a good story to tell,
Making your life purple
And your perfect tales, find their places

For your Future

To the soul that knows no fear
When your roots are deep

Everything that was in the past, let go
Be loyal to your present for your future

Silhouette

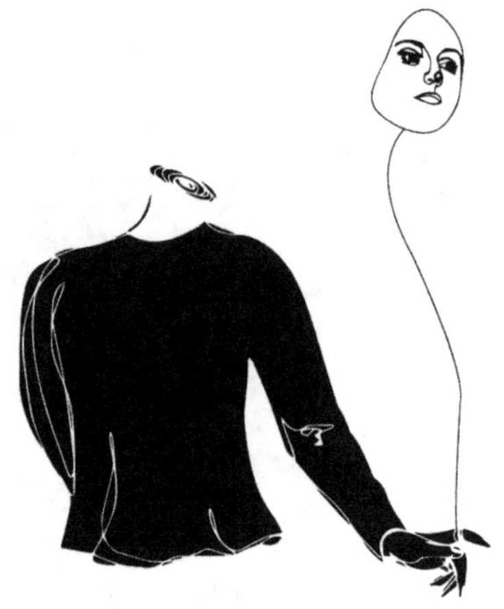

I've put up my wall,
Lest not tether yourself

I now do not crave to be found
Like Silhouettes of withered light

With the seated beliefs
Will they know, what they are missing out!

The Enchanting Moon

The moon
Casting its glow
and my camera primed
to capture its eternal beauty

The celestial enchantment
Taking me by sway
Like a lover so lost
in the splendor of one's beauty.

Come may what!

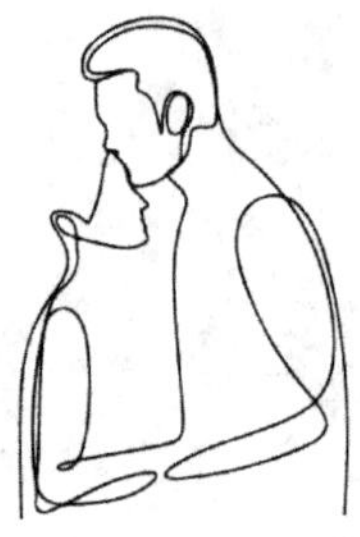

The best feeling I know
To be looked at
When you are looking away

To know that
My heart and soul are protected
Come may what!

A Garden in Bloom

There's a Garden in bloom
That's Desiring to blossom

Wishing to be Nurtured
Wanting to be Gardened

A garden left untouched for so long
To let it die is not what I wish for...

Your Home

The walls that you have built
To make it into a home of yours
The family you've created, so lovely!

Then why desperate enough
To destroy it down
With your own hands…

Tussle of Relation

Torn and tangled me,
Finding a key to remedy
Overthinking; keeping me occupied

Aren't you the most precious gift for your
parents,
Having them with you, as yours
We grow up, making them a bit wary

The tug between solitude and company
Time is ticking so quickly
To choose between wanting them or my reason

But never will you get the love you seek
In someone else, don't you think so,
The resting room after work, that you craved for
Tell me, will you get in anywhere else?

Serene bliss of love

The tussle of my virtue
From wanting everything
To not desiring anything.

Somewhere, wishing to break rules
To not cross the boundaries
But still wanting to taste that freedom

The serene bliss of love
That I long for, do I dream of it?
Shall I call for it, to be held in your arms?

Oh! The temptation I have
Of the conflicting desires
Calling for you, when I can't find you here!

Alone I lie in this Mess

Alone I lie in a mess of thoughts,
Scattered fragments, lost in thoughts
That the day has wrought;
In a tangled dress
Where dreams linger in the air, all around me…

Untouched by chaos, serene and rare.
In the night, as I lay
In the stillness, I find a quiet grace,
A solitary moment, a gentle embrace.
Where the heart speaks, and truth beholds.

Amidst the clutter, a clarity unfolds,
Alone I lie, yet not in despair,
For amidst the mess, there's a thought
A canvas of the growth I've painted myself
I gleam in awe, as I now have found pure gold.

Breath you take

The most difficult breath you take
Is the assurance called trust

The easiest of the breaths you take
Is of letting go of your soul in the name of
Grace!

Boon and Bane

The wish I made
Came true in the form of you
My love!

You are the boon
For the bane called me
Your love heals me.

My lonely calls for you

You are doing a lot
Actually, more than enough!

What if someone enters your life and says,
"Let us share the load, Down the road of life"...

Words, enough to caress my soul
Voice, enough to soothe my heart,

My lonely calls for you,
In my distress, your glance of assurance I seek.

95 per cent of the Universe

Something about you
Makes me wonder
Sometimes one's loneliness is beautiful

Just like the vast, unexplored
95 per cent of the Universe
Dark, seeking to be explored

Just like the lonely space surrounding you
Your mind meditating on the focal point
Calling your Consciousness to seek shelter
under Thee (My Almighty)!

Buds don't bloom before time

Sometimes modesty is dangerous
A mannered affectation

The insincerity I have dealt with
Made me learn to be pretentious

Like, the Buds don't bloom before time
Your conscience takes time to evolve.

Why I do things I do!

Judge me!
Oh, who are you to judge me,
What have you seen?
How much can you endure!

For you to say it's less
Have you encountered it
To not know how strong my heart is
How can you judge me!

The reason I do things that I do now
Feelings now that I hide somewhere
Cracks I'm trying to mend
That's me – how marred my journey has been till
now!

The due, I knew!

When your favourite person turns you down
That due was there, and your heart knew!

Your higher self knows you,
It will guide you well, out of the ruins

Love, not something I can force on you,
Frustrated enough, can't have all of it back

But it was due, and I did prepare for that,
The mountains – only I was supposed to climb!

What was I losing

You kept asking for forgiveness
I like a fool, kept giving it

Without counting, without knowing
What was I losing, my self-respect!

To realize and to stop feeling like a fool,
Believing no more in apologies

Now no need for crying over it
You don't deserve to be a part of my life!

Heartstrings

You wish me to be yours
As it's on you when you want me,
Guess, I am just a pawn of your desires
Like some heartstrings tethered.

Beyond the control of ours,
You test my resolve, as if I'm your belonging
Telling me to stay yours, never to leave
Moments do last, but these aren't the ones I wish
to stay

I let myself yield to its allure,
As if you are all I got
You probe my devotion to you,
as in a poet seeking truth in every line.

I cherished you in my heart,
But you had my heart in your hands
I belong to myself, but with you, I'm stringed
Your presence is all that my heart knows!

Just like a dream that fades away

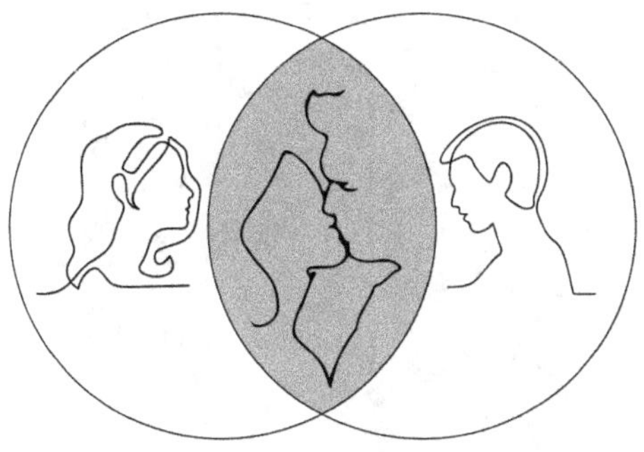

There's a lie I keep telling myself
Maybe they've had their reasons
They would've been suffering inside

Maybe I wasn't the best comfort
Maybe they would've been hurt in the past
Maybe I was meant to make y'all feel better

Maybe they were meant to come and leave
Just like a dream that fades away
That I always wanted to come true one day

Maybe he'll come back to me one day!

Star fire

Not everything is in your control
Let it go.

Don't burn your star fire
For what is unknown

Igniting light in the cosmic ties
Your beauty awaits to spellbound all.

I bow down to you

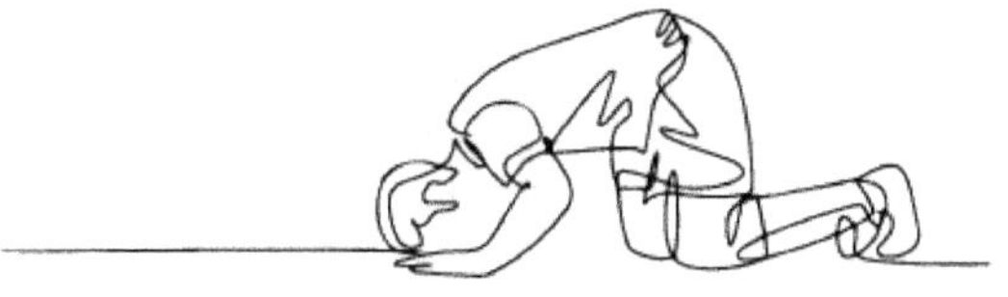

To the sun I bow down to,
Like the river that flows to the sea,
Gratitude for blessing me with this life
Me to witness beautiful mother nature!

For the air that I breathe
To the water, I quench my thirst
For every struggle, I go through,
you reward me with your existence!

The pain I had to endure,
my devotion grows stronger in you
For the decline of my righteousness,
you possess me with what I lack!

You fall and then you rise!

Character is made by what you stand for
Reputation is what made you fall

You don't give up when you lose or fall,
But until you are done with it, shall you rest?

Casualties in life can make lose sanity and
displeasure you,
But to taste it all, you fall and then shall you
rise!

A Fair Trail

What would you call being fair?
Does it mean to be right every time?
To always come up with solutions
To look out for the good that is hidden

It's a long way to oblivion
what we see is not the truth,
More to look behind the lies
truth that can unnerve you

Walking on the path of traces left
of someone who already crossed the lanes
But I strived to go ahead, choosing a new path
that never was trailed on...

Just like a Stardust

Where memories need you
To bring back the light

Like the stardust leaving traces
Your presence feels like that far-away star

The divine align of lines
To let us wither away together.

I want you to Remember

I'm still waiting for you to come back
Come back to the place we left each other
stranded
At the place, we said, "We will meet again."
But never went back
I'll be waiting, I want you to remember,
We still have ourselves to surrender…

Libra

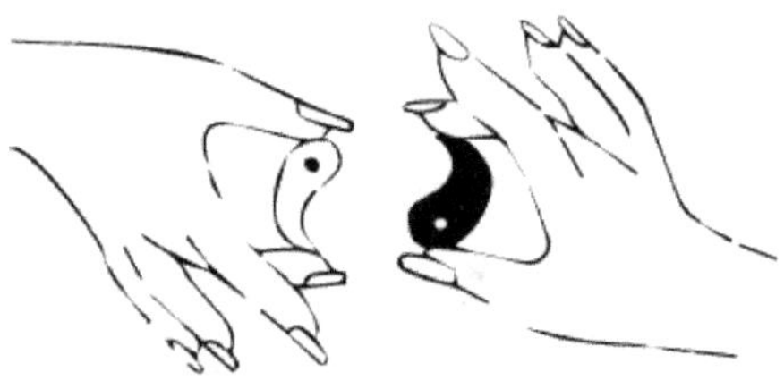

When you have too much to give
And All is taken from you
with a smile, you stand, your heart as vast as the
ocean
That's when you've found the real you

Get on my nerves, be in a good or bad way
Lay your head down to get the burden unladen
Give it a try; won't you try
Just unburden me from those hidden signs

Why are my thoughts unspoken?
Maybe they like to shelter up as pearls
Inside the Hardened layer of shell…
Waiting, Only to be shared when it's time, to the
Right person!

World on fire

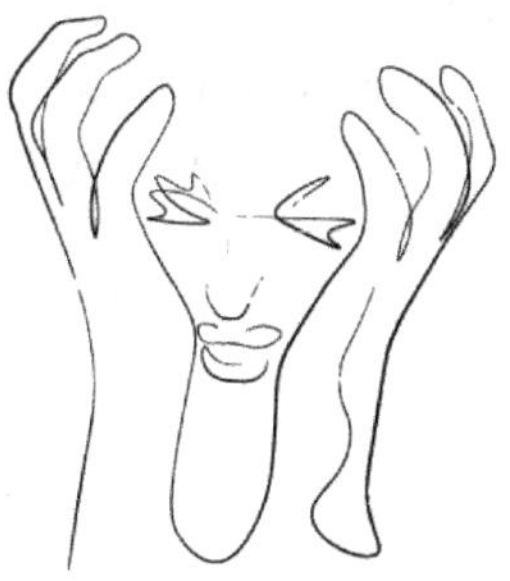

Where one's happiness lies
Somewhere on the cost of others
When humanity loses its way
That's where the world starts to burn

The power you grab
The emotions you curb
The freedom you take away
To increase your own

Nothing more than the boundaries
Nothing more than the suffering
Nothing much like one's freedom
As war is politics by other means

World will take note of chaos
The dance you do in the lives of others
Destroy the hard work, hard-earned fortune
Burning the cities and losing self-control

People (hypocrites) will talk only to blame
But turn away from when them is to be blamed
Is it the land that is responsible
Or you, humans, who can't learn responsibility?

Fire – that Purifies

Fire is proof that there is always hope
and it will burn all that is there to the ground.

To purify the evils in you and around
When the darkness within you overpowers your
serendipity

Your decisions are seen by all, like flames
spread afar
But never the choices to choose from, let them
know when it all ends

In the end, it's just bones and ashes

In the end
What is left of us...

Just our bones and ashes

Mother Nature accepts our remains
And Our souls detach itself

Live, love, serve, sacrifice; as you can't give
more time to your life
As Your life is just a memory in this vast
multiverse

Patience holds the key

Patience is a virtue,
and all good things come to those who wait!

When difficult times and situations surround
you,
One must stay calm! That's the key.

Circumstances change with time,
As change is constant in this world

Everything in life is pre-written
What is meant to happen will occur.

You may change the course of how you do
things!
And with prayer and true devotion, if you might;
can be re-written!